The voice of one Woman

METTABEL OKULAJA, MD

PRESS

www.xulonpress.com

Dedication

This book is dedicated to all the women who have
been, who are, and who will become all that the
Lord has created them to be.

To Anne,
God bless you for being
a blessing!

Mettabel
03/16/13
voice of onewoman@gmail.com

Acknowledgements:

My thanks go to my parents, Foluso (HOH) and Ojuolape (my one and only Olumae) Okulaja. Without you, I could not have been. To my siblings and their mates—Ademola, Olubukola, Olusola, Olamide, and especially Adeolu (the credit goes to him for the beautiful cover and back page photography)—you are a mixed bag, but I love you all.

Thanks to BBO. You made me believe that I could write this book, and for that, I am eternally grateful. Ojay Oluwole, my big sister, and Nancy Maggard (Mama Nancy), you both helped plant the seed for this work. OluB Mabo, you are and have always been the voice of loving truth in my head. Folake Olumide, you paved the way ahead of me and were not selfish about sharing. Toro Iluyomade, my Quiet Diva, and Christina Ajibesin, thank you both for the hours you gave to the first reading of my completed text. To Gwen Matthews (Mama Gwenche), my voice coach and friend of my heart, to Catherine Baier and Sele Akobo, my sister friends, and to Janet Boynes, fellow author, thank you all for taking the time to speak with and encourage me. I have been truly blessed by such great friends.

Pastor Tayo Badejoko, know that this chicken has become an eagle. Thanks, too, to my fellow sojourners, Kunle Oyekanmi and Motunrayo Adetola. Thank you, Olusesan Ekisola, thank you for constantly asking me, "Who is Mettabel?" To you, I say that this book is now part of the answer.

Many thanks go to Jennifer Hanchey, my editor, who made me look great in print. Your editorial input has truly been invaluable. To Pauline Buller, my illustrator, who translated the pictures in my head into the images that now grace this book and also helped with the formatting, thanks to you.

Thanks to the people who inspired me to write some of these stories. I cannot mention all of your names here, but my heart knows you all.

Most of all, I give thanks to God who saved me through His Son and showed me that I don't have to "do" to be His child; I just have to "be" His child. Thank you for making me Woman.

With much love from my heart,

Mettabel

P.S. Dreams really do come true!

Table of Contents:

Part I

The Source of:
Inspiration

in·spi·ra·tion [ɪnspɪ-reɪʃən]
- The stimulation of the mind or emotions to a high level of feeling or activity
- The quality of inspiring or exalting
- Divine guidance or influence exerted directly on the mind and soul of humankind*

*http://www.thefreedictionary.com

The source of all inspiration--according to what the Lord has shown me--is from God Himself within us. Many women have grown up broken and damaged, not seeing themselves as they really are, never understanding the fullness of what they have the potential to become. Sure, these women put on a brave face and keep on moving, but deep inside, they know that all is not as it should be. I for one have fallen into that category many a time, and through a series of divinely orchestrated events, I arrived at the place where I started to write what the Lord spoke to my heart, giving birth to what you now are about to read. Through the writing and creating of these poems, I have been inspired to see myself as a deliberate work of creation--not as a mistake. I have been inspired to see myself as woman, grown up from girl, imperfect but wholly beautiful. I have been inspired by these poems to enjoy who I am and look forward to who I want to, hope to, become. These thoughts challenge me to question and to rally against that "perfect" mold, the façade of modern womanhood our media sells. My desire is look to the Lord for my answers on femininity and worth instead of letting society form me. My true aim is to let Him be my inspiration.

Take a deep breath; your journey has also begun. I may not know where you are now or where your steps will take you, but destiny will lead you on. Let us walk together. Let's be inspired to see our womanhood as a gift and our beings as beautiful.

Mettabel Okulaja

The Journey to Becoming You

There are great gifts and talents
Encoded into the very essence of your being.
Never let anyone--least of all yourself--make you believe otherwise;
It would be the greatest lie you ever believed.

Unchain your mind and unleash your imagination from limitations
that bind.
They are the only glass ceiling preventing you from apprehending
your goals

Take every opportunity life presents you to express your gifting;
It may be the spark that lights up another life.

Take careful note of thoughts that cross your mind randomly.
One of those may be the key that unlocks the door to your dreams
coming true.

Be passionately passionate about your passions,
And protect them like a newlywed does his spouse.

Taking the first step towards your dream brings you a decade, a year,
a month, a week, a day, an hour, a minute, a moment closer to you
fulfilling destiny. Go ahead; start today.

Never base your perception of a matter on a negative cliché,
And also be wary of positive ones that predict a particular course of
events.
These are usually the products of the disillusioned mind,
Using them as a means to justify failures, or establishing them as
yardsticks for success.
The former limits and the latter sets boundaries based on another's
experience.

Forge your own path;
Write your own story.

The price you pay to achieve your dreams
Is like a great purchase made at basement bargain price.
The cost is often far less than the real value of the object
And is usually only available for a window of time--
Grab it while you can!

Tomorrow is another possession that does not belong to you;
Use what you have today--*Carpe Diem*!

Will to be who you want to be,
And you will become who you were meant to be.
Remember:
Nothing shall be impossible to him who believes.

I'm a Girl, and I Like It!

I'm a girl, and I like it!
I was created female,
Carved out and sculpted,
A brilliant work of art.
My depths and contours
Shadow the mystery within,
My hills and valleys a delight to behold.

I'm a girl, and I like it!
Prepared and hidden away for a season,
Incubated in the Master's kitchen,
Poured into my mould,
Baked to perfection,
Not a dimple in sight.

I am a girl, and I like it!
Brought by divine serendipity
To the one from whom I was cleaved,
Instinctively recognized and bonded.
Flesh of my flesh;
Bone of my bone.
Standing completed, yet still my own.

I'm a girl, and I love it!

A Moment in Time

I say a prayer inside my heart,
Nary a thought, an answer soon to come.

In astonishment, a moment in time,
My heart's desire fulfilled.
Through a mouth, not my own,
Heart to mouth, through a path walked by grace,

To prove to me that I am heard,
And that no thought is unknown to Him.

Actualization translated from dreams,
Played my principal, on the stage of the heart.
Open and naked all things He beholds,
Vision to life, by His breath infused,

To prove to me He sees and knows,
The center of me, the core, the source.

I stand in awe, in stillness, in hope,
Knowing that from heart to mouth He'll speak,
From thought to deed, He'll do.
The mystery of faith: His Word He will not break,

Time through time,
Till eternity unfolds.

Isaiah 65:24

"It shall come to pass
That before they **call**, I will answer;
And while they are still **speaking**, I will hear"
(emphasis added).

What secret thoughts and desires have you had that you thought were too big to verbalize in prayer? Think on this. Write of your desire, breaking it down into small, achievable segments. Pray over each segment, marking it off as you receive the answers to those requests.

_____

_____

_____

_____

_____

_____

_____

_____

_____

_____

_____

_____

_____

I Do

Ten flanking, resplendently matched,
Perfectly aligned, elegant in form,
The centerpiece entrancing,
Ying and Yang,
Fire and Ice,
Like the zebra, unashamedly entwined,
Mesmerizing mystery dance of ancient times,
Male and female made He them.

Poised for life,
I rise; I walk; I glide; I float.
Yet, with resolve, my goal in sight,
Neither faltering nor wavering.
For I must stand and say my piece.
Compelled by my love, it moves me on.
Head held high,
Heart pumping, blood pulsing,
Lips trembling, words tumbling.
In breathless wonder,
I whisper, "I DO."

Proverbs 30:18, 19

"There are three things that are too amazing for me,
four that I do not understand:
the way of an eagle in the sky,
   the way of a snake on a rock,
the way of a ship on the high seas,
   and the way of a man with a maiden" (NIV).

My Prayer: *"Aujourd'hui*.... "Engedi"***

Lord, this is my prayer today:
Expand my vision,
Deepen my understanding,
Prune my thoughts,
Breathe life into my dreams.

Extend my circle of influence,
My ability to source out all things good.
Cause me to be fruitful and productive
In all that I lay my hands to *do.*

Give me the power to *be,*
In the fullness of all I was created for.
Direct my paths;
Order my steps.

Make of me the hand
That lifts to uphold,
That opens to loosen
The stranglehold of poverty and lack.

My heart let overflow
With streams of liveliness and love.
Let ripples of laughter ricochet off my walls,
The joyful squeals of children from my halls.

Let me be a source of joy to my beloved,
Inspiring songs of praise to the most Beloved.
Let the dawn of each day bring with it rays of hope
That illuminate every crevice of discouragement and despair.

Let the Son of Righteousness arise,
With healing in His wings,
Causing elation to soar within
On wings of the wind.

Let the slide show of my past
Reflect images of time well spent.
Not of places to revisit,
But a rear view image,
A defining point, a reference--Engedi.
Setting a course for the future,
New vistas conquered.

Let satisfaction and rest be my endpoint,
The breath that sighs,
Deep calling to deep,
When You say, "Well done."

* Aujourd'hui – French word which means today.

**Engedi - En Gedi: "The Spring of the Goat" is a town on the west side of the Dead Sea in Israel. En Gedi is the place where David fled from King Saul. It is a place where four fresh water springs erupt from the desert wall and create an oasis of fertile ground for plants and animals. En Gedi has long been used as a place where desert travelers could come and rest, regain their strength, then move back out into the desert.

*www.bibleplaces.com/engedi.html

I Am She

I am She.
My name is Woman,
Female, Lady, Damsel,
All that embodies the completion of male.

I am She.
Color, shape, and form
Unique, every part of me
Irreproducible, "one of a kind."

I am She.
Black, white, latte,
Mochaccino, cappuccino,
Every creamy, delightful shade in between.

I am She.
Tireless worker, generous giver,
Faithful encourager,
Wholly encircling arms of love.

I am She.
Wife, Exquisite Lover, Faithful Friend,
Mother, Formidable Foe,
Fearless Protector of all her domain.

I am She.
Gentle and strong,
Graceful and poised,
Girlish coquette,
The mystery of God's creation,
A marvel, glorious to behold.

I am She.
Created by Genius,
Crafted with style,
Junoesquely statuesque,
Diva, Duchess,
The epitome of all things feminine.

I am She.
The curve of my breasts,
The sway of my hips,
The flow of my form,
Beautiful and altogether delightful.

I am She.
At the sight of me, you pause with pleasure,
My perfume wafting,
My texture pleasing,
My essence surrounding:
Inexplicable mystery.

I am She.
Look at me; learn me.
Touch me, and feel me.
Do not be afraid to *know* me.
I am She.

And forever destined to be for all of my time.

Genesis 2:23b

"She shall be called Woman,
Because she was taken out of Man" (KJV).

How Will My Heart Go On?

What do I do? Where do I go?
Oh, oh! How will my heart go on?
Truly I've loved and do still love.
In futility, though the heart be strong.
Why? I ask.
To what end or purpose achieved?

I cry inside, all held within,
For no right have I to wail aloud.
Turmoil within, roiling and rolling
Like labor pains; this must surely end.

A baby born or arms bereft,
Belly of emotion once swollen
With the promise of that to come.
Now collapsed, force of storm abated.

Nevertheless, this womb has held a soul,
A life that even now still lives on
In tangibility or in the sphere of realms unseen,
A spritely soul, a whispering.

Glad I am that I love and am loved.
Though out of sync,
What was now is
Perfectly attuned, encapsulated beyond time.

Pockets of happiness, discretely savored,
Giddy delight, silliness, joy,
Passion, heights soaring,
Melancholic, inspirational,
Deep.

But surely as the heart beats on,
The story of time
It's tale must tell,
To declare her His-story.

I wait and tell my heart to wait
For that which for which it must.
A shadow I see now,
Truly felt but elusive to touch.

Nebulous as mist in the new dawn
Lifts to reveal a new day, a new dream,
A new hope, A new love--
Made surer and stronger by that
Which within still burns.

YOU

You came into my life stealthily;
You stole into my heart.
You helped me see what I hadn't seen:
A child, a girl, a woman.

You looked at me when no one was looking.
You loved me, and yes and yes, I knew it.
You made me see my beauty as unique;
You drew out of me what I did not know I had.

You caused me to pull from deep within,
Out of the box and into the world--
A paradigm shift, A turning around.
Another chapter begun.

You spoke to me late into the night.
With you I learned to listen better.
You opened up the door of your heart,
Letting me in, letting me see.

You made my every matter yours.
A stranger once but surely no more,
You sang to me; you made me laugh.
The moment we stopped talking, I missed your voice.

With you my silliness was a delight,
My naïveté your constant amusement.
Yet through it all, I felt your strength,
Your faith in me, cheering me on.

When I cried, though you couldn't see me,
You heard my tears. I know not how.
You carried my burdens; yes, you did.
You made my every hurt your own.

You laughed with me and laughed at me,
And through it all, I learned to shift.
Many have not seen you the way I have.
That I cherish and always will.

I am changed because of you.
I am more "me" because of you.
My heart gives thanks to God for you.
I celebrate you as you've celebrated me.

And though these verses here end on paper,
They go on and on in my heart.
Thank you for being mine for time.
Thank you for being my friend.

There is one who loves deeply enough to leave an indelible print on the soil of the heart. Such a one should not be remembered with acrimony but with gratitude; for a heart that has not loved is no heart at all.

Mettabel

1 Samuel 18:1

"Now when he had finished speaking to Saul, the soul of Jonathan was knit to the soul of David, and Jonathan loved him as his own soul."

Mystique of Woman

The mystique of woman--
Oh, where has it gone?
Lost in a world of
"Bare all" and "Tell all."
Yet, in puzzlement behold
Woman, prime in her time,
Wholly discovered, cultivated, harvested.
All revealed; all sold, bartered, and traded.
Oh, the loss of mystique!

The loss of womanly appeal its own story tells:
Man constantly wanting;
Woman forever seeking--
A world of classifieds.
Pursuing the unknown yet familiar,
Surrendered in narcissistic wonder,
Their own reflections revered.
Defiant in their deviance
Against naturality.

Mystique of Woman:
Forever lost? Can we reclaim?

The worth of a vessel should not be measured by that which it
displays, but by what it contains.

Mettabel

The Remnant, The Seed

My strength is gone--
Dissipated, exhausted,
Swept away, of no use within,
Fit only for the waste without.
Yet bravely I stand,

As a seed caught in with winnowed chaff,
Dried up, forgotten, separated, isolated,
Thrown out and trampled under,
Discarded, abandoned,
No hope in sight.

Burned by the scorching sun,
Surely destined to die.
Swept of howling wind,
Of suddenness caught

On a wayfaring branch--
A sanctuary of sorts.
Oh, but soon displaced,
Separated, and once again alone.

Driven deep amidst the earth,
Pounded, pierced,
Surely the end is come.
Then suddenly peace!

Not a sound to be heard,
Surrounded by moist darkness,
Nothing seen, nothing. . .
By God! I feel my innards quiver,
Quickening from deep within.

Pulsing, throbbing,
Oh, it will not stop,
Nor would I will it to.
For my parts begin to move!

Now throttled from within,
I push, gaining strength,
Breaking forth to feel
No more the scorching sun,

But gentle warmth cradling the settled dew,
Cleansing, renewing--a bath to my soul.
I'm revived! I'm revived!!
From hands that stripped to arms that wrap,

By forces once gripped now with strength propelled.
My bruises healed;
My spirit raised.
No more death or dearth.

I'm revived! I'm revived! I'm revived!
I'm revived to live again!

Mosebolatan (Thought I Was Done)

Thought I was done,

Dissipated, discharged, and discomfited,

Dispersed, dispensed, and direly displaced,

Diverted, deflated, by default detained.

Demanding divine delimitation,

Dispensation, by detail delineated,

Dichotomy, divergence, definitively destroyed.

Destiny deferred; thought delayed.

Now, defined and duly displayed.

The Choicest

When things go awry,
Needs must to try.
When there is a breach,
Must be to reach,
Digging deep within,
Without intent to excuse,
Seeking one's self to recuse,
For no judge competent are we
In ruling of ourselves to stand.

For to be restored,
Needs must allow
The heart to be cradled,
Prodded and examined,
Peradventure there be
A crack to be filled,
A gap to be scaled.
Layers stripped away,
Laid raw and ready.
A wound to be salved;
A hurt to be healed.

Oh, that surely we would--
For then we would have gained
That which sundry seek but few attain:
A resting place.
Contain or display,
Neither the one more important.
The master's choicest unveiled,
The beauty of a vessel molded
And most excellently reformed.

More

There are things I do not have,
Many more I cannot reserve.
There are things I wish I could do,
And many more that I know I should.
But to build edifices to these--
That I have determined not my flesh to appease.

There are paths I have not traversed;
Many more my feet yet to tread.
There are things I do not own,
But incomparable treasures,
To me, have been made known.

For that which I have,
I, it behooves to appreciate.
Lest lust for more contaminate
All valued and cause to depreciate.

There are things I do not know,
Fewer still I understand,
But this one thing is clear to me:
If there's a tomorrow
(As sure there is),

There'll be more to see,
More to learn,
More to know,
To no more to own.
There'll be more to grow
And cause to flow,
From more, to more, to more.

And so resolve I to dwell,
Not on what has been or
Has not been,
What is or is not,
But to fix my gaze on that to come,
To moor on what my heart can see.
More and yes, by God, more.

31

I Am a Woman

I am a woman.
Steeped in femininity,
The princess, the pride and joy,
Mark of my Creator's divinity.

I am a woman.
Strong and sturdy in mind,
Soft and gentle in love,
A succor, my very own's delight.

I am a woman.
The beauty of my mothers
Through me shine.
In the integrity of my fathers,
I walk, indomitably tall.

I am a woman,
Indefinable, intriguingly complex,
My robe, my covering,
My glory, my wealth,
Draped around my elegant form.

Times have changed;
History's been made,
But neither pathos nor tragedy,
Poverty or wealth,
Oppression to emancipation
Can and will ever alter the fact
That. . .

I AM A WOMAN.

Part II

The Heart of:
Meditation

med·i·ta·tion [mɛdɪ-teɪʃən]
- The act or process of meditating
- A devotional exercise of or leading to contemplation*

*http://www.thefreedictionary.com

Meditation is the art of being able to tune in to conversations between the soul and the spirit. Inspired words are often the portals through which this communion can be reached. However, for meditation to effect change for eternal purpose, it must be animated by the most inspired words of all, the Word of Life that is able to transform. As we meditate, the veil of doubt, fear, and despair is removed, and all that seeks to mar our vision is swept away, allowing the light of revelation to shine upon mortal man and reflect the glory of our immortal God.

So, take a break. Sit a while, and enter into your private place. Let these words of life speak to you. Listen in to the conversations between *your* soul and *your* spirit, and write down what you hear. You may laugh; you may cry; you may sigh. But as sure as the dawn comes, you'll be changed.

A friend made is a good thing. A friend kept is better still. A friend loved is the best of all.

Mettabel

_____

_____

_____

_____

_____

_____

_____

_____

_____

_____

_____

_____

Proverbs 18:24

"A man who has friends must himself be friendly,
But there is a friend who sticks closer than a brother."

A palace does not a king make, but wherever a king lives is a palace.

Mettabel

_____

_____

_____

_____

_____

_____

_____

_____

_____

_____

_____

_____

Philippians 4:11

"Not that I speak in respect of want: for I have learned, in whatsoever state I am, therewith to be content" (KJV).

A picture, though said to be better than a thousand words, is still silent.

Mettabel

_____

_____

_____

_____

_____

_____

_____

_____

_____

_____

_____

Proverbs 25:11, 12

"A word fitly spoken *is like* apples of gold
In settings of silver.
Like an earring of gold and an ornament of fine gold
I*s* a wise rebuker to an obedient ear."

A rich life, like a musical score, is a symphony composed. It's not just about the melody, but about the message. A few notes do not an anthem make.

Mettabel

_____

_____

_____

_____

_____

_____

_____

_____

_____

_____

_____

Philippians 3:13

"Brethren, I do not count myself to have apprehended; but one thing *I do,* forgetting those things which are behind and reaching forward to those things which are ahead, I press toward the goal for the prize of the upward call of God in Christ Jesus."

Always let at least one night pass over a hurt or major issue. It might not seem so bad after all in the light of a new day, and you would have refocused on destiny by turning within.

Mettabel

_____

_____

_____

_____

_____

_____

_____

_____

_____

_____

_____

Ecclesiastes 7:8, 9

"The end of a thing *is* better than it's beginning;
The patient in spirit *is* better than the proud in spirit.
Do not hasten in your spirit to be angry,
For anger rests in the bosom of fools."

Just like the covenant of death came from eating fruit that hung from a tree, so the covenant of life came by the Bread of Life who hung from a tree.

Mettabel

_____

_____

_____

_____

_____

_____

_____

_____

_____

_____

_____

John 6:51

"I am the living **bread** which came down from heaven. If anyone eats of this **bread**, he will live forever; and the **bread** that I shall give is My flesh, which I shall give for the **life** of the world" (emphasis added).

Denigrating yourself, achievements, and/or your dreams--or giving room for anyone else to do the same--is tantamount to setting yourself on an excruciatingly slow head-on collision course, presenting your denigrator with a self-directed license to kill.

Mettabel

_____

_____

_____

_____

_____

_____

_____

_____

_____

_____

1 Timothy 4:12-16

"Let no one despise your youth, but be an example to the believers in word, in conduct, in love, in spirit, in faith, in purity. Till I come, give attention to reading, to exhortation, to doctrine. Do not neglect the gift that is in you, which was given to you by prophecy with the laying on of the hands of the eldership. Meditate on these things; give yourself entirely to them, that your progress may be evident to all. Take heed to yourself and to the doctrine. Continue in them, for in doing this you will save both yourself and those who hear you."

Even when it's raining on the inside, always let the sun shine on the outside, for your countenance is the image of your expectation.

Mettabel

_____

_____

_____

_____

_____

_____

_____

_____

_____

_____

_____

_____

Matthew 6:17, 18

"But you, when you fast, anoint your head and wash your face, so that you do not appear to men to be fasting, but to your Father who *is* in the secret *place;* and your Father who sees in secret will reward you openly."

We all dream of greatness, but greatness does not just come to where you are. You have to rise up to meet it.

Mettabel

_____

_____

_____

_____

_____

_____

_____

_____

_____

_____

_____

2 Timothy 1:6, 7

"Therefore I remind you to stir up the gift of God which is in you through the laying on of my hands. For God has not given us a spirit of fear, but of power and of love and of a sound mind."

Expect the unexpected manifestation of the expected. Expectation foreshadows experience. Expect new things. Prepare for change, and it will come--and maybe suddenly.

Mettabel

_____

_____

_____

_____

_____

_____

_____

_____

_____

_____

Acts 2:2

"And suddenly there came a sound from heaven, as of a rushing mighty wind, and it filled the whole house where they were sitting."

Greatness is birthed daily through pangs of tribulations and trials.
Joy adorns daily because of the determination to live life beautifully.
Innocence is reborn through divine refashioning of vessels of clay.
Life renews daily by the breath He breathes into our souls.
Understanding dawns with the breaking of each new day.

Mettabel

_____

_____

_____

_____

_____

_____

_____

_____

_____

_____

Isaiah 50:4b

"He awakens Me morning by morning,
He awakens My ear to listen as a disciple" (NASB).

46

He who is ruled by his environment will live a circumstantial life. He who disciplines himself to rule his environment will live an amazing and influential life, the stuff dreams are made of.

Mettabel

_____

_____

_____

_____

_____

_____

_____

_____

_____

_____

Romans 4:18-20

"Who, contrary to hope, in hope believed, so that he became the father of many nations, according to what was spoken, *"So shall your descendants be."* And not being weak in faith, he did not consider his own body, already dead (since he was about a hundred years old), and the deadness of Sarah's womb. He did not waver at the promise of God through unbelief, but was strengthened in faith, giving glory to God."

I have come to the realization that almost everyone I talk to leaves the conversation a little smarter than I because they've heard all I had to say. From now on, I plan to be the smarter one.

Mettabel

_____

_____

_____

_____

_____

_____

_____

_____

_____

_____

_____

_____

James 1:19

"So then, my beloved brethren, let every man be swift to hear, slow to speak, slow to wrath."

If you will give God a dime of every dollar you earn, He will make everything you desire in your life a dime a dollar, but if you do not, your dollar will not be able to get you anything worth a dime.

Mettabel

_____

_____

_____

_____

_____

_____

_____

_____

_____

_____

_____

Malachi 3:10-12

"'Bring the whole tithe into the storehouse, that there may be food in my house. Test me in this,' says the LORD Almighty, 'and see if I will not throw open the floodgates of heaven and pour out so much blessing that you will not have room enough for it. I will prevent pests from devouring your crops, and the vines in your fields will not drop their fruit before it is ripe,' says the LORD Almighty. 'Then all the nations will call you blessed, for yours will be a delightful land,' says the LORD Almighty" (NIV).

In the land of imagination and conception, dreams are born. Raw materials are gathered by revelation and sifted by meditation, revealing the hope of realization. As chaff is dispersed and substance settles, these elements, through Spoken Word inspired and fueled from within, focus on directed activity and action, within a divinely orchestrated milieu that results in the shift in entropy called *change.*

Mettabel

_____

_____

_____

_____

_____

_____

_____

_____

_____

Genesis 31:10-13

"And it happened, at the time when the flocks conceived, that I lifted my eyes and saw in a dream, and behold, the rams which leaped upon the flocks *were* streaked, speckled, and gray-spotted. Then the Angel of God spoke to me in a dream, saying, 'Jacob.' And I said, 'Here I am.' And He said, 'Lift your eyes now and see, all the rams which leap on the flocks *are* streaked, speckled, and gray-spotted; for I have seen all that Laban is doing to you. I *am* the God of Bethel, where you anointed the pillar *and* where you made a vow to Me. Now arise, get out of this land, and return to the land of your family.'"

Nothing is declared until it is spoken.

Mettabel

_____

_____

_____

_____

_____

_____

_____

_____

_____

_____

_____

Mark 11:23

"For assuredly, I say to you, whoever says to this mountain, 'Be removed and be cast into the sea,' and does not doubt in his heart, but believes that those things he says will be done, he will have whatever he says."

Once the log in one's eye is taken away, one will see that the speck in the other's is just that.--a speck.

Mettabel

_____

_____

_____

_____

_____

_____

_____

_____

_____

_____

Matthew 7:2-4

"For with what judgment you judge, you will be judged; and with the measure you use, it will be measured back to you. And why do you look at the speck in your brother's eye, but do not consider the plank in your own eye? Or how can you say to your brother, 'Let me remove the speck from your eye'; and look, a plank *is* in your own eye?"

Paradoxical to the world finite is the truth of life eternal.

Mettabel

_____

_____

_____

_____

_____

_____

_____

_____

_____

_____

_____

_____

Matthew 24:35

"Heaven and earth shall pass away, but my words shall not pass away" (KJV).

The degree to which true greatness can be achieved is dependent on the willingness to serve. A servant's heart with the Master's resources at one's disposal sets the stage for powerful things to happen.

Mettabel

_____

_____

_____

_____

_____

_____

_____

_____

_____

_____

_____

John 13:15-17

"For I have given you an example, that you should do as I have done to you. Most assuredly, I say to you, a servant is not greater than his master; nor is he who is sent greater than he who sent him. If you know these things, blessed are you if you do them."

The mark of one who will apprehend destiny: the willingness to allow God to interrupt routine life and to follow Him whenever, wherever.

Mettabel

_____

Mark 10:17-22

"Now as He was going out on the road, one came running, knelt before Him, and asked Him, 'Good Teacher, what shall I do that I may inherit eternal life?' So Jesus said to him, 'Why do you call Me good? No one *is* good but One, *that is,* God. You know the commandments: *"Do not commit adultery," "Do not murder," "Do not steal," "Do not bear false witness," "Do not defraud," "Honor your father and your mother."'* And he answered and said to Him, 'Teacher, all these things I have kept from my youth.' Then Jesus, looking at him, loved him, and said to him, 'One thing you lack: Go your way, sell whatever you have and give to the poor, and you will have treasure in heaven; and come, take up the cross, and follow Me.' But he was sad at this word, and went away sorrowful, for he had great possessions."

The one who finds it difficult to receive is so because he finds it even more difficult to give.

Mettabel

_____

_____

_____

_____

_____

_____

_____

_____

_____

_____

Acts 20:35

"I have shewed you all things, how that so laboring ye ought to support the weak, and to remember the words of the Lord Jesus, how he said, It is more blessed to give than to receive" (KJV).

The thoughts of the heart, like a maze, are understood by none but the originator, and the blueprints are accessible to none other than the one to whom the rights are released. To attempt to navigate them or force a way through would be an exercise in utter futility--until that heart finds a place of comfort to rest, breathe, and release.

Mettabel

_____

_____

_____

_____

_____

_____

_____

_____

_____

1 Corinthians 2:10-12

"But it was to us that God revealed these things by his Spirit. For his Spirit searches out everything and shows us God's deep secrets. No one can know a person's thoughts except that person's own spirit, and no one can know God's thoughts except God's own Spirit. And we have received God's Spirit (not the world's spirit), so we can know the wonderful things God has freely given us" (NLT).

To enquire is not to err, but to assume is to blunder--and sometimes quite terribly.

Mettabel

_____

_____

_____

_____

_____

_____

_____

_____

_____

_____

_____

_____

_____

Proverbs 18:13

"He that answereth a matter before he heareth it, it is folly and shame unto him" (KJV).

What is seen is the most changeable form of existential matter. It too shall pass.

Mettabel

---

2 Corinthians 4:18

"So we fix our eyes not on what is seen, but on what is unseen. For what is seen is temporary, but what is unseen is eternal" (NIV).

Faith is tangibility pointing to the infallibility and immutability of the intangible.

Mettabel

_____

_____

_____

_____

_____

_____

_____

_____

_____

_____

_____

Hebrews 6:18, 19

"That by two immutable things, in which it is impossible for God to lie, we might have a strong consolation, who have fled for refuge to lay hold upon the hope set before us: Which hope we have as an anchor of the soul, both sure and stedfast, and which entereth into that within the veil" (KJV).

We are who God says we are. Whether we are or not is a matter of where in the continuum of time and morphogenesis; But the truth remains unchanged, even if as yet undiscovered. We are who we are.

Mettabel

_____

_____

_____

_____

_____

_____

_____

_____

_____

_____

Romans 8:29

"For those whom He foreknew [of whom He was aware and loved beforehand], He also destined from the beginning [foreordaining them] to be molded into the image of His Son [and share inwardly His likeness], that He might become the firstborn among many brethren" (AMP).

With God impossibilities are an impossibility!

Mettabel

_____

_____

_____

_____

_____

_____

_____

_____

_____

_____

_____

_____

Mark 10:27

"And Jesus looking upon them saith, With men it is impossible, but not with God: for with God all things are possible" (KJV).

When you love who you are and are passionate about what you do, you will not need a daily alarm clock to propel you to start your day. Your passion will awaken you; your passion will move you; your passion will motivate you; your passion will drive you; your passion will propel you; your passion will define you; your passion will inflame you, excite you, fulfill you, strengthen, establish, satisfy, and settle you. You never get weary. A fire always burns within.

Mettabel

_____

_____

_____

_____

_____

_____

_____

_____

_____

_____

Jeremiah 20:9

"Then I said, I will not make mention of him, nor speak any more in his name. But his word was in mine heart as a burning fire shut up in my bones, and I was weary with forbearing, and I could not stay" (KJV).

Part III

The Muse of:
Reflection

re·flec·tion [rɪ-flɛkʃən]
- The act of reflecting or the state of being reflected
- Mental concentration; careful consideration
- A thought or an opinion resulting from such consideration*

*http://www.thefreedictionary.com

That which reflects who we really are is the true mirror of our souls. We may not like what we initially see, but as we keep looking, we will eventually see what we like.

2 Corinthians 3:18

"But we all, with unveiled face, beholding as in a mirror the glory of the Lord, are being transformed into the same image form glory to glory, just as by the Spirit of the Lord."

My Life to Live

Is this the life I'm meant to live?
Is this all I've got to give?
These are questions
I ask myself
And the One who wrote
This saga that's called
"My Life."

Sometimes I'm sure;
Sometimes I'm not.

But surely as I live and breathe,
I always wonder, and I do wonder,
Am I the "me" I'm meant to be?
Or was I created for more to see?
Oceans to cross,
Mountains to climb--
Not of paper and work,
Daily and drudge,
But of places and people.

Purpose and destiny,
Purpose and destiny.

These are the words that reverberate.
And so as I strive to not perseverate.
I'll keep going to that secret place,
To seek and search, To see His face.
That I may know which way to take.
Finally this thirst to slake.

That at the end,
At the end,

I may triumphant entry gain.

New but Known

I speak aloud as heard I write.
I move; I start, beginning.
The voice, my familiar, though course uncharted be.
Destination unknown, but not in vain pursued.
Uncertainty made sure;
Steps established and firm.

I have not come this way before,
But like a gazelle, with grace my steps
Are led to places seen within--
Images framed by faith to be
Scripted indelibly, role by role,
Themed constant, unwaveringly.

Words: translated, transfigured, transformed,
Breathed into,
Becoming flesh alive.
Intangibility made tangible; hope realized.
I see, I feel, and now I know
As I am known, for sure to be.

Ponder

No one is born perfect.
No one has it all.
There are many questions not answered,
Many answers questioned.

God is revealed in every circumstance,
Through turbulence, trials, and triumphs.
The future He unveils, without limits, without fear--
A legacy of faith, a covenant of trust.

Between God omnipotent and man wholly impotent
A bond is forged.
Molding, unleashing, straining, breaking forth,
The rebirth of beauty in life, our universe, our world.

The miracle of recreation,
Once again revived.
A new heart once again beats
In sync with purpose and destiny.

From water to life,
From tears to joy,
From despair to fulfillment,
From defeat to victory.

Yes, has not God said,
"Fear not, for I am with you;
I will help you.
Yea, I will strengthen you.
Yea, I will uphold you
By My mighty right hand"?

Fear not!
There is hope!
Do not look down;
Do not despair.
Square your shoulders; lift your chin up high,
Knowing that He is your glory and the One who lifts your head,
Knowing that He will never fail you, nor forsake you,
Knowing that He is with you, and you *will* win--
Always.

Once Blind, Now I See

The roar of silence,
The voice of the mute,
The timbre of the falls,
The resonance of the echo,
Fear of the secret,
Gaping chasm within--

This place so deep
That none but the bold therein venture:
My mind. This is the place I go
Where none dare follow,
None dare sleuth.
Battles fought; battles won.
Agony and pain, once neighbors there,
Foreclosed and evicted.

Now, contentment resides.
The flow of the waters,
The bubbling of the springs,
Thirst quenched,
Forever assuaged;
Satiety attained.

By living water drenched,
Cleansing deluge,
Purifying torrent,
The clay washed away.
Once blind, now I see.

I Must

I must. Must I?
Oh, yes! I must.
Must?. . .Must !
Where must I?
How must I?
Why must I?
Because I must. . .
I must?
Yes! Must be that I must.
Must be?
Must be.
I must have to. . .
I want; I will; I must.
I do.
I must want to will to do.
I must.
That I will to do. . .
I trust He must will for me to do.
Help me, Lord, to do what I must.. . .

For I must!

Listen

Listen, making sure to hear.
Hear again until understood.
What is understood to be done, do.
After you've done, wait.
While waiting, cogitate.
Through cogitation, deconstruct.
Then listen--again.

Who?

He was suave; he was fly.
Spoke to me real softly,
Dulcet tones seducing,
His voice wrapping
As with whipped butter,
Tantalizingly smooth
In textures and tones.
Behind the veil, his face concealed.

By senses drawn,
Primed and ready.
"Do it my way,"
With a whisper to ease,
Cool as the evening breeze,
His breath on my skin,
"This way, please,"
No shuffle or shift.

Not here, yet not there.
Anticipation, perseveration,
Vivid imagery conjuring, alluring,
Perpetual slideshow aimed to entice.
Then suddenly, illumination,
Another calling from within:

"Remember, remember. . .
The veil is to be removed
Wherein the truth now be revealed."
Pulling back, as the wind blew away
That which had heretofore been concealed,
Inscribed and embedded,
Forehead clearly now seen,
Revealed by the light of day.

The word, the name:

SIN.

Think

Think: What does it profit?
Gain the world; lose your soul.
Worldly fame and fortune crossover not.
Naked you came; naked you go.

What will you say
To the one who created, called, and sent
When He questions and requires your answer?
Stuttering excuses, "Um ...um... um,"
or glorious report, a life *well* spent?

THINK, THINK, THINK!
And decide today
If you will hear His voice.

The men, women,
The guys, and the gals
There to cheer you on:
"You go, girl! You're the man!"
But, alas, inadmissible evidence
In the court of the Lord.

No popularity contest, plaques,
Money, cars, houses, *stuff--*.
Clearly no room for those
In the cubicle six down below.
Transition they cannot achieve,
Useless as currency discarded
Beyond its "sell by" date.

What will you do
When alone you stand?
You will, you know.
Stand tall, or cower in shame?
Rejoice, or stand horrified
At the residue of your tried works?

Remember: no communication
Between hither and thither.
No cameras, lights, action!
It's real, baby; it's real.
This is IT

Life is short; like a mist,
It vanishes away.
But when the mist clears,
Reveals the light of a new day,
What will you see?
A glorious new day,
Or. . .

Lay hold of what is eternal.
Listen for the voice of the commander,
And march to the beat of your destiny.
You're on your way,
Child of God.

He waits,
Victorious child of God.

Dunamis

I think:
If I am silent, I will never be heard.
If simple, be overlooked.
And if restrained, be void of effect.

By a still, small voice, I have learned:
In silence is more power than mere words;
In simplicity, more impact profound;
In restraint, greater strength unleashed,
The essence of "I Am" unveiled in me.
Power, Impact, Strength: Dunamis.

John 3:8

"The wind blows where it wishes, and you hear the sound of it, but cannot tell where it comes from and where it goes. So is everyone who is born of the Spirit."

Isaiah 30:15

"In returning and rest you shall be saved;
In quietness and confidence shall be your strength."

Dunamis is an Ancient Greek word meaning "power" or "force".
http://www.thefreedictionary.com

Part IV

The Passion of:
Expression

ex·pres·sion [ɪk-sprɛʃən]
- The act of expressing, conveying, or representing in words, art, music, or movement
- Something that communicates
- The manner in which one expresses oneself, especially in speaking, depicting, or performing
- A facial aspect or a look that conveys a special feeling
- The act of pressing or squeezing out*

*http://www.thefreedictionary.com

I'll tell you a bit about the thoughts that make me me, and maybe someday I'll get to hear what makes you you.

Methinks that the Lord is trying to tell us something;

What do you think?

One of my patients once came in for her annual appointment; and because she had been a patient of mine for a while and she was comfortable with me, we began talking.

"I have had a really good year," she said, "that's why I haven't been in. What with three grandchildren and all. . .thanks to you."

"Me?" I said.

"Yes, you," she replied. "You remember what you told me when I told you my daughter was having a hard time getting pregnant?"

Whoosh! The story came back to me, and I tell it here with permission.

This patient of mine had come in, and being the "touchy-feely" doc that I am, I noticed that she seemed kind of blue. "What's the matter?" I asked her.

"It's my daughter. She is not in a good place right now because she wants a baby so badly. She has tried in-vitro five times, and she just got the news that the last one did not take."

I spent some time talking to her, but it then occurred to me that although commiseration is fine, I had something more to give her. I could gift her with faith to believe for a miracle. I said to her, "Please, don't think that I'm weird, but would you please tell your daughter to do something?"

"What do you want me to tell her?"

"Tell her to say to herself every morning, ' I am a mother; I was created to bear children. My body will carry a child to birth. I was meant to have a child.'"

"Oooh, I don't know if she'll go for that. She doesn't believe like that, but hey, she has nothing to lose, so I'll tell her." The patient left my office shortly afterward, looking only slightly better.

A few months later, my patient came back for a follow up visit, and at the end of the office visit, she said, "I have a surprise for you." She put her hand in her purse, brought out a piece of paper, and handed it to me. It was an ultrasound image of a baby!

"Is this what I think it is?" I said excitedly.

She nodded and said, "Yes! I'm going to be a grandma!"

"Wow!" I said.

"You know, after you spoke to me, I went to my daughter's house and shared with her what you asked me to tell her. She was very skeptical, but I mentioned it to her a few times, and then she said, 'Okay, Mom, they're only words, so okay, I'll do it. . .I have nothing to lose.' I tell you, Dr. O, she made those confessions faithfully every day. They still went through the in-vitro process, but this time it took! After eight years, it took, and look at this picture. Isn't he beautiful?"

"Yes, he is," I answered, overwhelmed with gratitude to God. Those "mere words" gave birth to (as of the time this story was written), a 19-month-old miracle. Halleluiah!

Mark 11: 22-24

"Have faith in God," Jesus answered. "Truly I tell you, if anyone says to this mountain, 'Go, throw yourself into the sea,' and does not doubt in their heart but believes that what they say will happen, it will be done for them. Therefore I tell you, whatever you ask for in prayer, believe that you have received it, and it will be yours" (NIV).

Give yourself or someone a gift of faith today, and watch your words grow to fruition.

Hush, Little Baby

I just sat there and watched helplessly as the tears rolled down her face. At sixty years old, she has never been married. Oh, no, no man would ever have the opportunity to lord it over her.

Her father had just died. He was ninety-five years old; he had had four wives, a few children, and step-children. Half laughing, she said, with a bitter-sweet twist to her mouth, "There were no mourners at his farewell parade." For, he'd done it so many times before, and he paid. Oh, yes, he paid, but at what cost?

We talked a little more, and as she got up to leave, she gave me a hug and said thank you, but I could not see why, for I had not and could not have done anything to help what occurred fifty-five years ago.

Sitting at home mulling this over, I put pen to paper and wrote these words, an adaptation of an old nursery rhyme:

Hush, little baby.
Don't say a word.
Papa's gonna buy you
A little doll.

This little doll says,
"NO, NO, NO,"
But papa's gonna buy you
A pretty dress.

This little dress,
All tattered and torn,
Papa's gonna have to tell
A little tale.

This little tale,
Oh, so, so sad.
Papa's gonna take
A trip away.

Hush, little baby.
Don't you cry.
Papa cannot see
Your brand new dress.

You see, my friend had been abused as a child; her life terribly marked by this abominable act. She had suffered greatly, only recently having come to terms with the fact that she was not to blame for her father's actions. She had never really known the love of a father, neither had she been saved from this horrible situation by the people she thought would protect her.

There are many wives and young women--I dare say infant girls--out there who are being abused daily: sexually, physically, and mentally. Their lives and their spirits, broken by the very ones who should have nurtured them. If you have a mother, a sister, a wife, a girlfriend, fiancée, or--most of all--if you have a daughter, take the time to pray for her today that God will keep her safe and away from such evil, and for those who have been exposed, that the God of heaven would heal them completely. Also, please remember in prayer the many victims of such abuse, that the balm of Gilead would heal them and that God's spirit would help them find their way home, to find rest in the Lord's arms as my friend has done.

It started when she was five years old and ended when she became a "woman." He went to jail a few times, for he did this heinous thing again and again. Yes! That's what the stepdaughters were about.

So, please pray today, and don't be afraid to *speak out* if you see this happening. You might be saving a life. Let us pray:

"Hush, little baby, don't you cry, for my friend, I celebrate your freedom in Christ today. He has wiped the tears from your eyes. He has given you beauty for ashes, the oil of joy for mourning, the garment of praise for the spirit of heaviness (Isaiah 61:3). May you be blessed always".

David, David. . . A Man Like David

David, David, David: a great man, a flawed man, a shepherd, a king, a lover, a father, a priest, a warrior, a repentant man, a dynasty's beginning, a sinner, a murderer, a liar, an adulterer, a musician, a poet, a friend, a leader, a visionary, a worshipper, an unashamed chaser after God, a mentor, a brother.

Yes, yes, and yes, he was all these things and more. Many have thought and said, "How can God love such a man? For this man was so imperfect, with so many shortcomings. Yet, this man, *this man*, God loved and chose to establish His throne forever. What qualifies him so to be so special?"

You see, yes, he sinned and was a sinner; he messed up royally (pardon the pun). But this man David--as many as his sins were--when he did repent, he did so with sorrow, godly sorrow. He then never looked back to his sin; rather, he turned to God and embraced Him boldly and fully and without shame, just as if he had *never sinned!*

What awesome trust in God's forgiving grace and unending love. How can a father not love such a son who implicitly trusts in his sonship and who honors his father in that he never committed the same sin twice, *never?* And he never looked back, *never.* And once forgiven, he never cowered, never hid himself from God, *never.* Rather, he laid himself bare and trusted Him who had said, to do what He said.

What have you done? Have you sinned, lied, stolen, cheated, hurt, or abused another? Call upon God, the Father; repent and receive His love. Then, don't look back; hold your head up high and never let anyone or anything convince you that you are anything less than loved--absolutely, totally, crazily, as only God can.

I've been there and done that too, but no more--no more doubt. I am the redeemed, the beloved, the covered, the forgiven, and so are you. Yes, YOU!

So join with me today to celebrate Papa's love. Old things have passed away and behold all things have become new (2 Cor. 5:17b). I am my beloved's, and He is mine (Song of Sol. 6:3a) His banner over me was love (Song of Sol. 2:4b)

That's just the way it is; Things may not always be the way they seem.

Sam. What can I say? He was the most beautiful guy my twenty-one-year-old eyes had ever seen: tallish, mocha skin, and a killer smile. I was an intern at the University Teaching Hospital. The first time I saw him, he was flirting with the nursing students, and it seemed that every time I saw him, he was always walking aimlessly around the medical ward, chatting up girls and generally clowning around. I really didn't know why he was always around, but he just always was. A few months passed by, and I occasionally would see Sam and would always make some pithy statement about him. I just didn't like him, for no apparently clear reason. He seemed so cocky and so full of himself.

On the first day of my internal medicine rotation, we were assigned patients, and life went on as usual. Then, one day, a new patient appeared on my list. His name was Sam Thomas. (Note: I had seen Sam around but did not yet know his name.) When I finally discovered this patient was the same man, I was at first surprised because I had never seen him in a hospital gown. To prepare myself for rounds and familiarize myself with the case, I picked up his chart and got a huge shock. This golden boy, this Adonis, was dying! He was in the final stages of acute leukemia, and his bone marrow, the part of the bone that produces blood, had burnt out. His only hope of staying alive was the transfusions that he had to have every three to four weeks, while hoping against hope for a miracle.

I was devastated. And I felt horrible for misjudging this man. He was only trying to make the best of a very bad situation. You see, he was an only child, and his dad was not in the picture, so his mom was the only constant support he had. However, he didn't let that get him down. Instead, he was always trying to make other people laugh and always had a smile on his face.

I cried that day, but I had to dry my tears because I had a job to do. I was on my internal medicine rotation for three months. Some of the time, Sam was my patient, and at others, I just took care of him while I was on call. Needless to say, we became quite close and developed a deep friendship. I was privileged enough to be a part of the process that led to him accepting Jesus into his heart. I would sometimes go just to visit, and we would spend hours just talking-- about our faith, about life.

Sadly, Sam didn't get better, despite all the treatments and prayers. After a while, he just stayed admitted because his need for transfusions was growing. One day I got called to the floor because a patient was not doing well. It was Sam. He had developed complications and was not expected to live much longer. There was not much I could do, but we talked until he could no longer speak. I just held his hand, and I don't know whether it was a few hours or a lot of hours, but Sam died that night. He didn't look too pretty, but his face was so beautiful because he died with a smile on his face.

I know I will see Sam again someday. But as I remember him today, I remember a courageous, generous, and beautiful child of God, and I remind myself that not all that seems to be is. The real miracle was the beauty of Sam's life and all the people he touched with his laughter and with love.

So, Sam Thomas, I remember you with love today, and I celebrate all twenty-two years of your life. You touched my life for all time. Salute, my friend. *I will* see you again.

** This is a true story, but the names have been changed to preserve privacy.

My "To Be" List

This is a true account.

I was browsing on the net the other day, and I saw a slammin' pair of summer sandals that had me salivating on the spot. I immediately clicked on the sandals--ladies you know how this can be--and behold, the site was sold out in my size. I went to the home site for that store, sure that a pair would be available, but no. I persevered: Amazon, nada; Zappos, zippo; Shoebuy, none to buy. I went back to the original site and considered ordering the next size down, but something curious happened at that time. The Spirit of God impressed it on my heart to go to their brand store located in a nearby mall the next day and told me that I would find the shoes in my size there. I gave the thought mental assent, but I actually forgot about it until, through a series of unrelated events (serendipitous I would call it), I was going to be eating at a restaurant close to that mall with a friend. Just as we were about to leave for the restaurant, the Lord reminded me again: The Mall of America. The location was really off the beaten path for me, but since I was going to be in the area, I begged my friend to allow me to go to the store before going to the restaurant. This is the scene that unfolded:

"Hi. I'm looking for a pair of sandals you guys had on line." I described the sandals.

"Ohhhh," the saleslady said, "we're sold out. They were really popular."

"I know," I responded, "it seems that the only size left on line in any kind of quantity is size five."

I was about to leave the store when another saleslady said, "Wait! What size would you like?"

"Well, a size nine," I said.

She said, "A lady just returned these shoes in size nine about an hour ago."

The customer had bought them online and returned them to the store. I was struck speechless; then I went "jibber-jabbery," telling the sales lady how I came to be at that spot at that time.

"Wow!" she said. "God told you you'd find the shoes here?"

"Yes," I said, my face almost splitting with a smile. "You see, God had reserved that last of a pair for me!"

I did take my shoes home with me that night, elated not only because I had gotten the shoes but because God had reserved them for me.

Note: In my shopping life, this is not a strange occurrence. It happens quite frequently, and a dear friend of mine always teases me that I'm the only one she knows who says that the Spirit led her to score a deal.

"So," she said, "Mettabel, what does this tell you about things you've asked for that have seemingly not manifested in the physical?"

We then had the conversation that led to me meditating and coming up with the "To Be" list below, which is my list of how to *be* while we're waiting for the manifestation of what He has done.

My "To Be" List:

1) Be Specific: Tell God exactly what you want, and don't make Him have to do a daily crossword puzzle on your requests. Dig deep into His Word and your heart, and tell Him what you want.

2) Be Bold: Set your sights high and do so without apology.

3) Be Expectant: Believe. Even if the answer seems to be delayed, it will come in its own appointed time.

4) Be Thankful: Know that He is faithful to do what He has promised.

5) Be Hopeful: For hope preserves promise; don't be discouraged.

6) Be Steadfast: Decide to be immoveable, always abounding in the work of the Lord and keeping your profession of faith, for surely you *will* receive the promise.

7) Be Vigilant: To check on your progress and your position, examine yourself and see whether thou still be in the faith; activate your spiritual GPS.

8) Be Watchful: To see and hear what He will say to you, guard your heart with all diligence.
(We all need this!)

9) Be Discerning: Be perceptive, and you will be able to recognize when your desire is manifested and your blessing revealed.

10) Be a Witness: Testify of the Lord's goodness when the promise is fulfilled; open up your hand and bless another.

I share my "To Be" list with you today so that it may be a blessing, just as I was blessed.
P.S. My story is for the guys too--sometimes you shop more than we gals do!

Seasons and Times

Seasons and times: they teach us what the Word tells us, that there is a time for everything.

We often look at spring as the beginning and winter as the end of the seasons, but the lining up of the seasons with creation and nature demonstrates that winter actually represents the beginning, a time of hibernation and incubation when everything appears cold, dreary, and desolate--sometimes dismally vacuous. But underneath the barrenness, in actuality, there is life! Like a pregnancy waiting to be birthed, beneath the surface, beneath the freeze, winter is active. When it looks like nothing is happening, it is in actuality the time when the greatest ground in morphogenesis is covered.

The life cycle of the butterfly illustrates this concept beautifully as it shows us that the most pivotal, developmental stages of the egg and most of the pupal stage are hidden and accomplished within dark and cramped confines. During these stages, changes are occurring and processes are being refined. These processes are so critical to the final emergence of the mature butterfly, that to attempt to shorten or externally facilitate the timeline of the process--either through sympathy, desperation, impatience, or any other preemptive emotional stimuli or actions--may result in the termination and abortion of the life that is being incubated.

The next season is spring. Spring may be likened to the emerging of the chrysalis, the great thaw, the "coming out." It's unarguably the most exciting of all the seasons, a time of release from confinement or custody, a time to unveil that which has been ensconced; it is a flowering. Ultimately, spring is the most awe-inspiring part of the seasons of life as this is the time when the most dramatic *visible* changes occur, a sharp divide between apparent barrenness and fruitfulness.

Then comes summer: the Butterfly stage. This is a time of blooming, vividness, and abundance. Truly, summer's bounty is the cornucopia of life. The thesaurus offers the following synonyms for summer: heyday, prime, acme, zenith, efflorescence, flowering, blossoming, fructification (www.thefreedictionary.com). Summer is when movement is the fastest, colors are the brightest, and sounds are the most intense. The passing of time is barely perceptible, obscured by the flurry of constant activity. If pollination and seed gathering are not accomplished at this time, the stage will not be set up for an encore. This is the season in which spices of the past, present, and future are mixed together in vivid kaleidoscopic abundance. It is, however, also a time of planning and execution for the continuance of life. Summer is a time to "seize the day".

Then finally autumn brings different hues that are no less vibrant. The sunset of life which--contrary to the concept of fizzling out--is depicted by nature as a fiery blaze of glory, the season of the golden hues. Autumn is a time of harvesting and reaping, a time of reward, synchronous in nature, an allegorical representation of the symbolic. Note that I do not refer to this season as fall. Originally, this term was used to depict the falling of leaves, portraying a decline (a function which I do not believe it was meant for). Rather, autumn is a release for the next season, a preparation for the time to come.

For a life to come into being, there must be copulation, fertilization, embryogenesis, fetal maturation--all unseen. Then the seen breaks forth with birth, growth, development--physical, mental, spiritual and sexual--and again, copulation. The cycle of life continues, with each stage having its time. So, live it! It's called your life! Your pace may be different from mine, and your summer may be my winter, but we all go through the seasons.

The most important message is to celebrate whatever stage you are in. Own it. Let the Creator's timeline be yours also. There is a time for everything, and whether the season is summer, winter, springtime, or harvest, know that everything has its time.

Ecclesiastes 3:1-8

"To everything there is a season,
A time for every purpose under heaven:
A time to be born,
And a time to die;
A time to plant,
And a time to pluck what is planted;
A time to kill,
And a time to heal;
A time to break down,
And a time to build up;
A time to weep,
And a time to laugh;
A time to mourn,
And a time to dance;
A time to cast away stones,
And a time to gather stones;
A time to embrace,
And a time to refrain from embracing;
A time to gain,
And a time to lose;
A time to keep,
And a time to throw away;
A time to tear,
And a time to sew;
A time to keep silence,
And a time to speak;
A time to love,
And a time to hate;
A time of war,
And a time of peace."

Ecclesiastes 3:11
"He has made everything beautiful in its time. Also He has put eternity in their hearts, except that no one can find out the work that God does from beginning to end."

Why do I write this? I write because I perceive that many, like I, have come into, have gone through, or are in a winter season of their life. I write to encourage you that though no eye has yet seen, nor ear heard, nor entered into the heart of man what is brewing within you, God knows, for He is the one working within you (Phil 2:13 For it is God who works in you both to will and to do for *His* good pleasure). Begin; start; commence; come into being, and come into existence; arise; see the light of day; give birth; shine and prosper. Your time is coming. It is here. The butterfly emerges; new life begins.

Honey, I Shrunk Myself!

For many years, whenever someone would pay me a compliment--for instance, about something I had on--instead of saying a simple thank you, I would shrug the compliment off saying, "This old thing?" If people admired something I owned, I would attempt to minimize the value for fear of seeming extravagant and unholy. I was always trying to make excuses for who I was and was forever trying to convince people that I was humble and holy, even though (I am now sure) no one was trying to make me seem vain or worldly.

Then as the Holy Spirit began to minister to me through experiences in my relationships with great and not so great friends (the latter have their uses too), I came to the realization that in all these interactions I was trying to minimize myself for fear of being thought grandiose.

Yes! The root was **FEAR**: fear of rejection, fear of condemnation, fear of being thought to be proud, fear of inadequacy. . .just plain fear. I discovered that I had become my own greatest judge and worst critic, and in becoming so, I had actually placed myself in a place that God had not intended for me to be. Therefore, I was living below my potential. No matter what good things others said or thought about me, I couldn't receive it because I saw myself as small in my own eyes. I had shrunk myself!

In legalistic and religious circles, this trait might be called humility, but the Lord showed me that in His Kingdom this false humility actually gives the enemy a chance to use the seemingly innocuous (and superficially religious) to effect heavy damage, prevent forward movement in the strength of the Lord, and keep us focused on ourselves and our "so-called" failings.

Consider with me the ten spies of Israel who were sent to survey the Promised Land. They came back acknowledging the beauty and richness of the land God had promised them. However, they then turned around and shrunk themselves by giving in to fear. The Lord had made them grand, but they turned their gaze inward, focusing on their perceived inadequacies. This self focus caused them to give up their chance to inherit the promise. Contrast this attitude to that of Joshua and Caleb who said, "We are well able to overcome [the land]" (Numbers 13:30). They did not even mention the name of The Lord at the time, but their confidence in themselves was in what God said about them. That divine assurance oozed out of their pores. While many of the other Israelites might have said the two men were proud, God had this to say about Caleb: "But My servant Caleb, because he has a **different spirit** in him and has followed Me fully, I will bring into the land where he went, and his descendants shall inherit it" (Num. 14:24, emphasis added). And The Lord also said concerning them in Numbers 14:38: "Of the men who went to explore the land, **only** Joshua son of Nun and Caleb son of Jephunneh survived" (NIV, emphasis added). Why? Because they believed what the Lord had said concerning them; therefore, they viewed themselves as able. This confidence was not found in their brothers. Numbers 13:33 records the spies' fear: "we saw the giants (the descendants of Anak came from the giants); and we were like **grasshoppers** in our own sight, and so we were in their sight" (emphasis added). They shrunk themselves, and they remained shrunken!

I share this so that those of us who were so deceived (no longer!) in the past will begin to accept ourselves the way God made us – full of great treasures! And in reality, our so-called quirks and the attributes that make us unique may actually be the stones that God will use to pave the path to our destiny.

I use mundane examples from my own life, but I speak of an essential truth: unless we see ourselves in the light of the Word and as God sees us--perfect through the sacrifice of His son Jesus--we will continue to live below potential. However, if by His grace and by the power of the Spirit we see ourselves in His truth, we will UNSHRINK ourselves! Honey, stop shrinking yourself!

Romans 8: 1, 2

"There is therefore now no condemnation to those who are in Christ Jesus, who do not walk according to the flesh, but according to the Spirit. For the law of the Spirit of life in Christ Jesus has made me free from the law of sin and death."

I Am. . .

Not defined by where I'm from.

I will. . .

Not be defined by how I look.

I am. . .

Not defined by what I have.

I will. . .

Not be defined by what I've done.

I am. . .

Not defined by what I see.

I am. . .

Me,

Defined by who I am.

I am Mettabel,

Favored of God.

Tell me who you are.

Part V

The Unveiling:
Revelation

rev.e.la.tion [rɛvə-leɪ ʃən]

- The act of revealing or disclosing
- Something revealed, especially a dramatic disclosure of something not previously known or realized.
- *Theology*: A manifestation of divine will or truth*

*http://www.thefreedictionary.com

It Is Finished

I give credence to the pain you've been through,
But TODAY I stretch forth my hand to pull you up.
For silver and gold have I not,
But all that I have I give.
To see you leap for joy once more,
To see you praise, and dance, and laugh.

I have been in the dark with you.
That impotent place called 'Land of despair'.
I wrestled and won, fought and prevailed,
With power today, I call you COME FORTH!
The time of death is passed,
And surely you shall live again.

For Lo with the morning coming,
Rises the Sun of Righteousness
With great healing in His wings.
To flood with light and love and LIFE,
My redeemed, for whom great price was paid.

You shall return sorrow and sighing fleeing away.
You shall arise; you shall alight.
Though you thought yourself forsaken
With my "It is finished" in death,
Your "life" gloriously begins.

So I lift you up and raise you high,
Oh! Forever on eagles wings
YOU SHALL FLY!!!
Your youth renewed, your strength restored
Though you were dead,
Yet shall you LIVE!

I received a mandate to write what I heard the Lord say to me and to send it out. This I have done.

Revelation 1:11

"I am the Alpha and the Omega, the First and the Last,"[f] and, "What you see, write in a book and send *it* to the seven churches which are in Asia:[g] to Ephesus, to Smyrna, to Pergamos, to Thyatira, to Sardis, to Philadelphia, and to Laodicea."

You are liberated, free to begin writing your own story--starting here, starting now. You are free to dream, free to live, and free to be all you can be. Congratulations and welcome to the next chapter of this epic saga called "Your Life."

Begin another chapter. Write your own story, the revelation of who *you* are!

The Beginning ...

2 Corinthians 3:17

"Now the Lord is the Spirit; and where the Spirit of the Lord is, there is liberty."

Revelation

_____

_____

_____

_____

_____

_____

_____

_____

_____

_____

_____

_____

_____

_____

_____

_____

_____